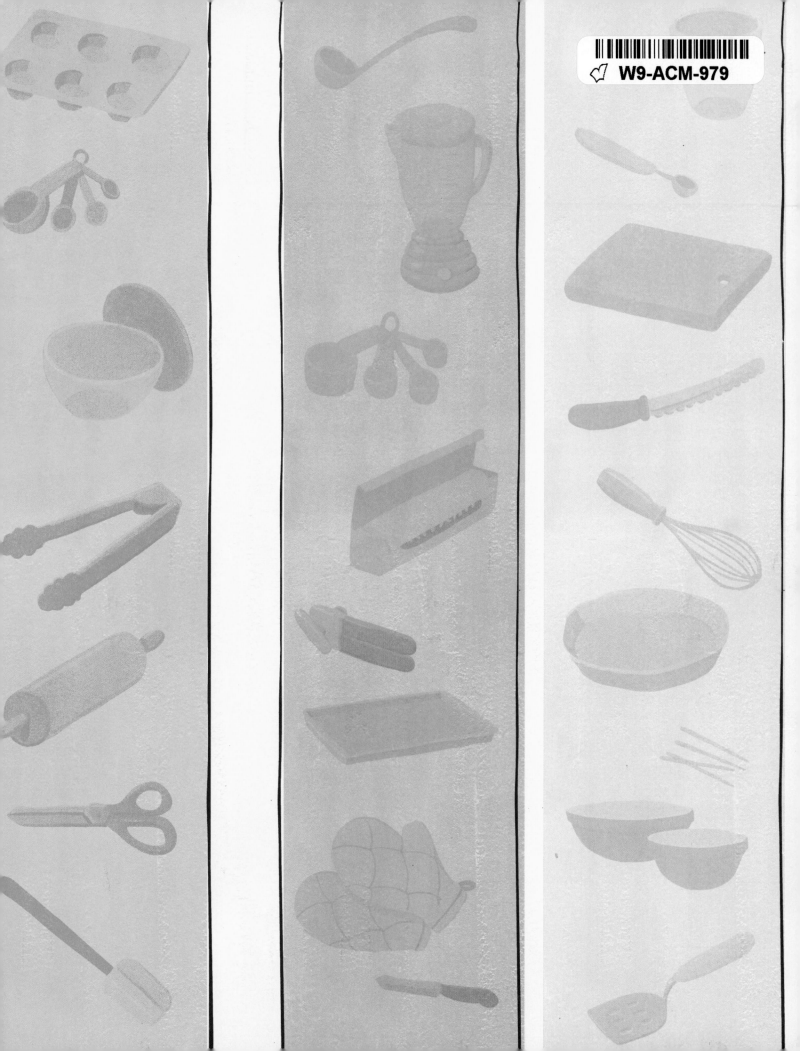

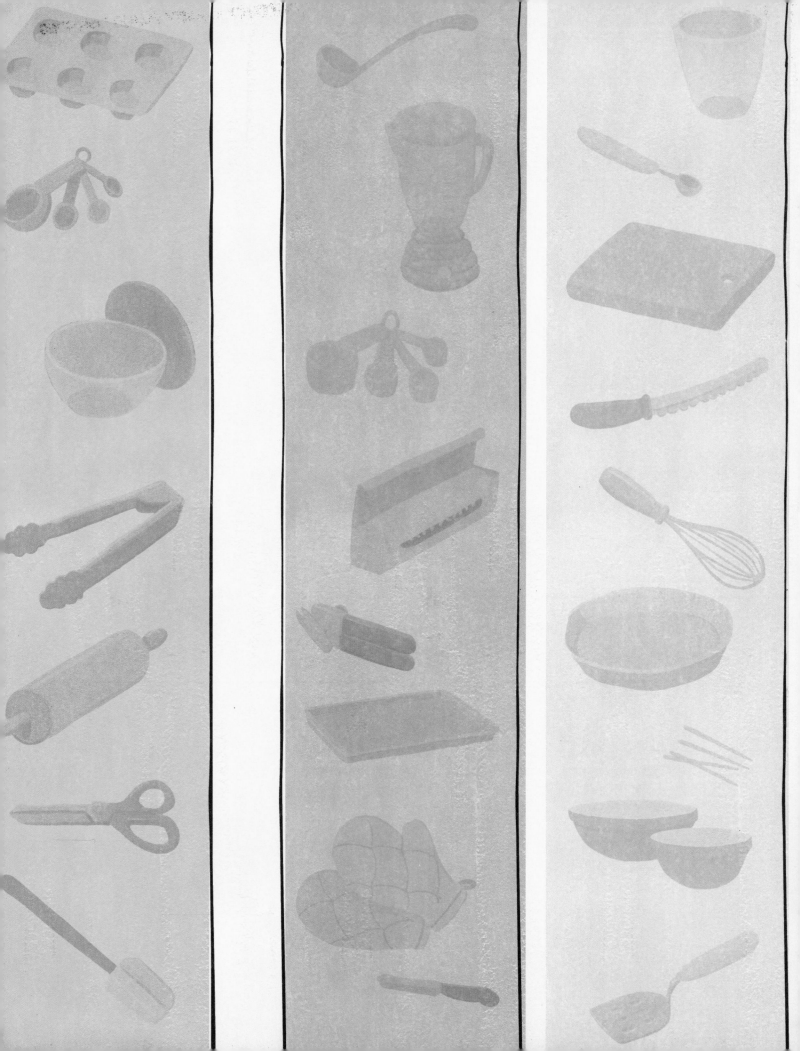

Walk-Around Tacos

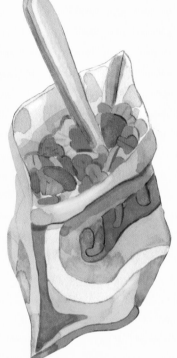

and Other Likeable Lunches

by Nick Fauchald   illustrated by Rick Peterson

Special thanks to our content adviser:
Joanne L. Slavin, Ph.D., R.D.
Professor of Food Science and Nutrition
University of Minnesota

PICTURE WINDOW BOOKS
Minneapolis, Minnesota

Editors: Christianne Jones and Carol Jones
Designer: Tracy Davies
Page Production: Melissa Kes

Art Director: Nathan Gassman
The illustrations in this book were created with acrylics and gouache.

The illustration on page 5 is from *www.mypyramid.gov.*

Printed in the United States of America

 All books published by Picture Window Books are manufactured with paper containing at least 10 percent post-consumer waste.

Library of Congress Cataloging-in-Publication Data
Fauchald, Nick.
Walk-around tacos : and other likeable lunches / by Nick Fauchald ; illustrated by Rick Peterson.
p. cm. — (Kids dish)
Includes index.
ISBN-13: 978-1-4048-3999-1 (library binding)
1. Luncheons—Juvenile literature. I. Peterson, Rick. II. Title.
TX735.F387 2008
641.5'3—dc22
2007032909

Editors' note: The author based the difficulty levels of the recipes on the skills and time required, as well as the number of ingredients and tools needed. Adult help and supervision is required for all recipes.

Table of Contents

EASY

INTERMEDIATE

ADVANCED

Nick Fauchald is the author of many children's books. After attending the French Culinary School in Manhattan, he helped launch the magazine *Every Day with Rachael Ray*. He is currently an editor at *Food & Wine* magazine and lives in New York City. Although Nick has worked with some of the world's best chefs, he still thinks kids are the most fun and creative cooks to work with.

Dear Kids,

Lunch is a very important meal. It gives you the fuel to keep going until supper. The recipes in this book were made especially for beginning cooks like you. They are also easy to pack-and-go.

Cooking is fun, and safety in the kitchen is very important. As you begin your cooking adventure, please remember these tips:

★ Make sure an adult is in the kitchen with you.
★ Tie back your hair and tuck in all loose clothing.
★ Read the recipe from start to finish before you begin.
★ Wash your hands before you start and whenever they get messy.
★ Wash all fresh fruits and vegetables.
★ Take your time cutting the ingredients.
★ Use oven mitts whenever you are working with hot foods or equipment.
★ Stay in the kitchen the entire time you are cooking.
★ Clean up when you are finished.

Now, choose a recipe that sounds tasty, check with an adult, and get cooking. Your friends and family are hungry!

Enjoy,
Nick

KIDS DISH

Note to Adults:

Learning to cook is an exciting, challenging adventure for young people. It helps kids build confidence, learn responsibility, become familiar with food and nutrition, practice math, science, and motor skills, and follow directions. Here are some ways you can help kids get the most out of their cooking experiences:

• Encourage them to read the entire recipe before they begin cooking. Make sure they have everything they need and understand all of the steps.

• Make sure young cooks have a kid-friendly workspace. If your kitchen counter is too high for them, offer them a stepstool or a table to work at.

• Expect new cooks to make a little mess, and encourage them to clean it up when they are finished.

• Help multiple cooks divide the tasks before they begin.

• Enjoy what the kids just cooked together.

MyPyramid

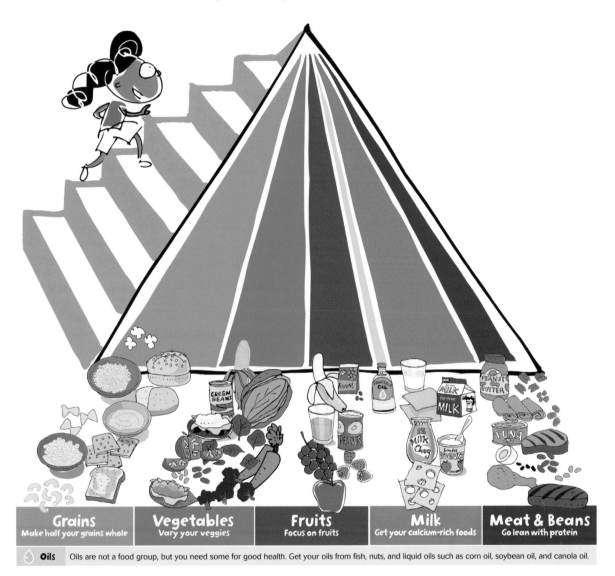

Grains	Vegetables	Fruits	Milk	Meat & Beans
Make half your grains whole	Vary your veggies	Focus on fruits	Get your calcium-rich foods	Go lean with protein

💧 **Oils**   Oils are not a food group, but you need some for good health. Get your oils from fish, nuts, and liquid oils such as corn oil, soybean oil, and canola oil.

In 2005, the U.S. government created MyPyramid, a plan for healthy eating and living. The new MyPyramid plan contains 12 separate diet plans based on your age, gender, and activity level. For more information about MyPyramid, visit *www.mypyramid.gov*.

The pyramid at the top of each recipe shows the main food groups included. Use the index to find recipes that include food from the food group of your choice, major ingredients used, recipe levels, and appliances/equipment needed.

Special Tips and Glossary

Cracking Eggs: Tap the egg on the counter until it cracks. Hold the egg over a small bowl. Gently pull the two halves of the shell apart until the contents fall into the bowl.

Measuring Dry Ingredients: Measure dry ingredients (such as flour and sugar) by spooning the ingredient into a measuring cup until it's full. Then level off the top of the cup with the back of a butter knife.

Measuring Wet Ingredients: Place a clear measuring cup on a flat surface, then pour the liquid into the cup until it reaches the correct measuring line. Be sure to check the liquid at eye level.

Bake: cook food in an oven

Chop: cut food into small pieces of similar size

Cool: set hot food on a wire rack until it's no longer hot

Cover: put container lid, plastic wrap, or aluminum foil over a food; use aluminum foil if you're baking the food, and plastic wrap if you're chilling, freezing, microwaving, or leaving it on the counter

Drain: pour off a liquid, leaving food behind; usually done with a strainer or colander

Drizzle: lightly pour something over the top

Layer: to stack things one at a time

Preheat: turn an oven on before you use it; it usually takes about 15 minutes to preheat an oven

Roll: flatten with a rolling pin

Slice: cut something into thin pieces

Sprinkle: to scatter something in small bits

Stir: mix ingredients with a spoon until blended

Stuff: to pack one item into another item

Toss: mix ingredients together with your hands or two spoons until blended

Whisk: stir a mixture rapidly until it's smooth

METRIC CONVERSION CHART

1/4 teaspoon (1 milliliter)
1/2 teaspoon (2.5 milliliters)
1 teaspoon (5 milliliters)
2 teaspoons (10 milliliters)
4 teaspoons (20 milliliters)

1 tablespoon (15 milliliters)
2 tablespoons (30 milliliters)
3 tablespoons (45 milliliters)
4 tablespoons (60 milliliters)

1/4 cup (60 milliliters)
1/3 cup (80 milliliters)
1/2 cup (125 milliliters)
2/3 cup (160 milliliters)
1 cup (250 milliliters)
2 cups (500 milliliters)
4 cups (1 liter)

6 ounces (168 grams)
8 ounces (2245 grams)
15 ounces (420 grams)

TEMPERATURE CONVERSION CHART

350° Fahrenheit (175° Celsius)
375° Fahrenheit (190° Celsius)

Kitchen Tools

Baking sheet

Blender

Butter knife

Can opener

Cutting board

Kitchen shears

Large serving bowl

Measuring cups

Measuring spoons

Mesh strainer

Microwave-safe bowls

Mixing bowls

Oven mitts

Paper towels

Paring knife

Plastic wrap

Rolling pin

Rubber spatula

Serrated knife

Whisk

Spoon

Toothpicks

Tongs

Wooden spoon

7

This Recipe Includes

GRAINS, MILK, MEAT & BEANS

Super Hero Subs

INGREDIENTS

1 loaf Italian bread
1/4 cup creamy Italian
　salad dressing
3 roasted red peppers
　from a jar
4 lettuce leaves
6 slices salami
4 slices bologna
4 slices American or
　provolone cheese

TOOLS

Serrated knife
Cutting board
Measuring cup
Paper towels
Medium Bowl

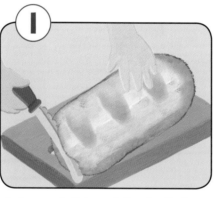

Ask an adult to cut the loaf of bread lengthwise.

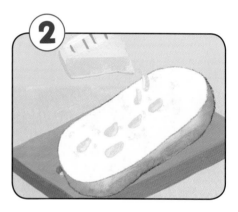

Drizzle the salad dressing over the top half of the loaf.

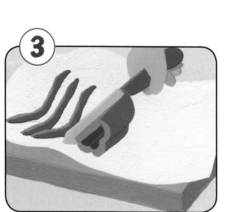

Drain the red peppers on a paper towel and have an adult cut the peppers into thin strips.

Wash the lettuce and tear it into pieces.

8

5

Layer the salami, bologna, cheese, lettuce, and red peppers on the bottom half of the loaf.

6 Cover the layers with the top half of the loaf and ask an adult to slice the loaf into four sandwiches. Serve.

9

This Recipe Includes
FRUITS, MILK

Go Bananas Smoothies

INGREDIENTS

1 banana
6-ounce container
   low-fat vanilla yogurt
3 tablespoons creamy
   peanut butter
5 ice cubes
1 teaspoon honey

TOOLS

Butter knife
Cutting board
Measuring spoons
Blender
4 glasses

1 Peel the banana and slice it with the butter knife.

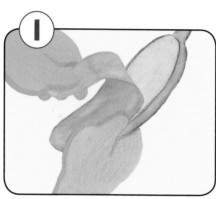

2 Dump the yogurt, banana slices, peanut butter, and ice cubes into the blender.

3 Cover and blend on medium speed for about 1 minute or until smooth.

4 Pour the mixture into four glasses, drizzle honey over the top, and serve.

10

NUTRITION NOTE★ Bananas are high in potassium, which helps your muscles and nerves work as they should.

Walk-Around Tacos

1

Open the chili and pour it into a medium microwave-safe bowl. Ask an adult to heat the chili for about 1 minute or until warm.

2

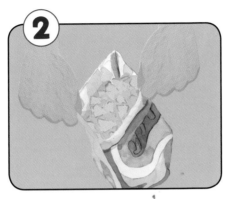

Open each bag of chips.

3

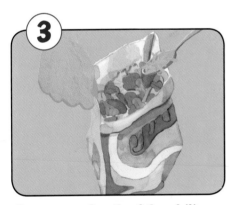

Spoon one-fourth of the chili, salsa, sour cream, lettuce, and cheese into each bag of chips.

4   Shake and serve immediately.

INGREDIENTS
15-ounce can chili
4 snack-size bags corn
   or tortilla chips
1/2 cup salsa
1/3 cup sour cream
1 cup shredded lettuce
1/2 cup shredded cheddar
   cheese

TOOLS
Can opener
Medium microwave-safe
   bowl
Measuring cups
Large spoon

11

MILK, VEGETABLES

Ranch Round-up Salad

INGREDIENTS

1 cup low-fat plain yogurt
2 teaspoons apple-cider
  vinegar
1/2 teaspoon onion powder
1/4 teaspoon garlic powder
Pinch of salt
Pinch of ground
  black pepper
8-ounce bag lettuce
4 cups assorted salad
  mix-ins, such as
  grated carrots, croutons,
  cherry tomatoes, and
  cucumbers

TOOLS

Measuring cups
Measuring spoons
Medium mixing bowl
Whisk
Large serving bowl
Tongs (or 2 spoons)

1 Place the yogurt, vinegar, onion powder, garlic powder, salt, and pepper into a medium mixing bowl and whisk them together to make the dressing.

2 Place the lettuce in a large serving bowl.

3 Drizzle a small amount of dressing over the lettuce and toss, using tongs or two spoons.

4 Add the salad mix-ins and more dressing to taste, toss again, and serve.

12

This Recipe Includes
GRAINS, MILK, MEAT & BEANS

Ham and Cheese Roll-ups

INGREDIENTS
4 slices whole wheat bread
4 teaspoons honey mustard
4 slices deli ham
4 slices Swiss or
   American cheese
4 dill pickles

TOOLS
Serrated knife
Cutting board
Rolling pin
Measuring spoons
Butter knife
Toothpicks

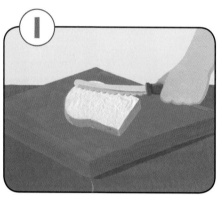

1 Ask an adult to cut the crusts off each slice of bread with a serrated knife.

2 With a rolling pin, roll out each slice of bread until it is flat.

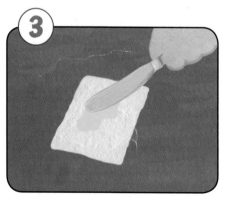

3 Spread 1 teaspoon honey mustard on each slice of bread.

4 Layer a slice of ham, a slice of cheese, and a pickle on top of the honey mustard.

HEALTHY CHOICE★ Try using turkey instead of ham and shredded carrots instead of cheese for a lower fat roll-up.

5

Roll up the bread and fasten each roll with three toothpicks, evenly spaced.

6 Ask an adult to cut each bread roll between the toothpicks to make pinwheels. Serve.

MEAT & BEANS, VEGETABLES, FRUITS

Tuna Stuffed Tomatoes

INGREDIENTS

6-ounce can of tuna
4 tomatoes
2 stalks of celery
1 scallion
1/4 cup ranch dressing

TOOLS

Strainer
Small bowl
Can opener
Serrated knife
Cutting board
Spoon
Paper towels
Paring knife
Measuring cups
Medium mixing bowl
Wooden spoon

Place the strainer over a small bowl. Open the tuna and drain contents through a strainer.

Ask an adult to cut the top off each tomato using the serrated knife.

Use a spoon to scoop out the inside of the tomato to form a cup. Flip the tomatoes upside down on paper towels to drain.

Ask an adult to chop the celery and scallion into small pieces.

HEALTHY CHOICE★ Serve with whole grain crackers for extra fiber.

5 Place the tuna, ranch dressing, celery, and scallion into a medium mixing bowl and stir together.

6 Stuff each tomato with one-fourth of the tuna mixture and serve.

17

GRAINS,
MEAT & BEANS

Nutty Butter Triangles

INGREDIENTS
2 cups honey roasted peanuts
2 tablespoons canola oil
8 slices whole wheat
    bread
4 tablespoons jelly or jam
    (your favorite flavor)

TOOLS
Measuring cups
Blender
Rubber spatula
Measuring spoons
Butter knife
Serrated knife

1 Pour the peanuts into a blender. Cover and blend the peanuts on high speed for 1 minute.

2 Turn the blender off and use the rubber spatula to scrape down the sides of the blender. Cover and blend again for 1 minute. [NOTE: Peanuts should be finely chopped.]

3 Add the oil and blend again for 1 minute, until the oil and peanuts are combined.

4 Spread 2 tablespoons of nutty butter on four pieces of bread.

18

NUTRITION NOTE★ Peanuts are rich in protein, which is important for building strong bones and muscles.

5

Spread 1 tablespoon of jelly over the top of each slice of nutty butter bread. Place a slice of bread on top.

6 Cut each sandwich into triangles and serve.

19

This Recipe Includes

VEGETABLES, MEAT & BEANS

Chicken Salad Lettuce Wraps

INGREDIENTS

6-ounce can chicken breast
  chunks
1 stalk celery
1 small sweet pickle
2 tablespoons mayonnaise
1 tablespoon sour cream
1 tablespoon chopped
  parsley leaves
4 large leaves lettuce

TOOLS

Strainer
Small bowl
Can opener
Paring knife
Cutting board
Measuring spoons
Small mixing bowl
Wooden spoon
Paper towels

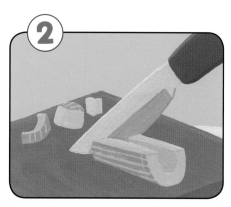

Place a strainer over a small bowl.
Open the chicken and drain it
through a strainer.

Ask an adult to chop the celery
and pickle into small pieces.

Place the mayonnaise, sour
cream, parsley, pickle, celery,
and chicken into a small
mixing bowl and stir together
until completely blended.

Wash and dry the lettuce
and place one-fourth of the
chicken salad mixture on top
of each lettuce leaf.

20

HEALTHY CHOiCE★ Make these wraps even healthier
by using low-fat mayonnaise and sour cream.

5

Roll the lettuce around the chicken salad to make four wraps.

6 Serve.

GRAINS,
MEAT & BEANS

Egg Salad Pita Pockets

INGREDIENTS
1 stalk celery
4 hard-boiled eggs
1/3 cup mayonnaise
1 tablespoon Dijon mustard
Pinch of salt
Pinch of ground black
    pepper
4 slices cooked bacon,
    crumbled
2 whole-grain pita bread
    rounds, halved
4 lettuce leaves

TOOLS
Paring knife
Cutting board
Measuring cups
Measuring spoons
Medium mixing bowl
Wooden spoon
Whisk

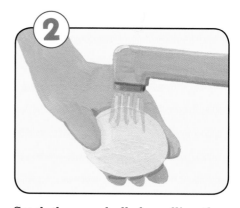

Have an adult chop the celery into small pieces.

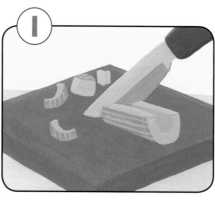

Crack the eggshells by rolling them lightly on the counter. Peel the eggs and rinse them under cold water to wash off all of the shell pieces.

Have an adult chop the eggs into small pieces.

Place the mayonnaise, mustard, salt, and pepper in a medium mixing bowl and whisk together.

22

5

Add the eggs, bacon, and celery and stir until combined.

6 Stuff each half pita round with a lettuce leaf and one-fourth of the egg salad. Serve.

23

This Recipe Includes

GRAINS, MEAT & BEANS

Hot Dog Pizza Boats

INGREDIENTS

4 hot dog buns
4 hot dogs
1 cup pizza sauce
1/2 cup shredded pizza
    cheese blend

TOOLS

Baking sheet
Paring knife
Cutting board
Measuring cups
Oven mitts

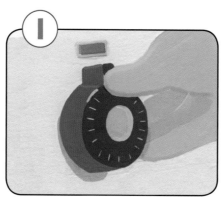

Preheat oven to 350°.

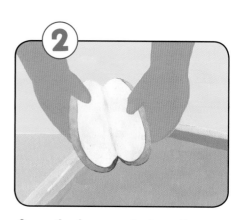

Open the buns and place them on a baking sheet.

Ask an adult to cut each hot dog into 1/2-inch slices.

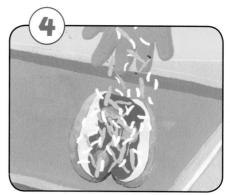

Layer the inside of each hot dog bun with slices of one hot dog, 1/4 cup pizza sauce, and 2 tablespoons of cheese.

24

HEALTHY CHOICE★ Hot dogs made with turkey, chicken, or vegetables are lower in fat and calories than those made with beef and pork. Read the labels to make the best choice.

5

Ask an adult to bake about 5 minutes or until the cheese is melted and the buns are slightly toasted.

6 Place the pizza boats on plates and serve.

This Recipe Includes

GRAINS, MILK, MEAT & BEANS

Puffy Pizza Rolls

INGREDIENTS

8-ounce can refrigerated
   crescent rolls
24 slices pepperoni
2/3 cup shredded
   mozzarella cheese
1 cup pizza sauce

TOOLS

Measuring cups
Baking sheet
Oven mitts
Plastic spatula
Small microwave-safe bowl

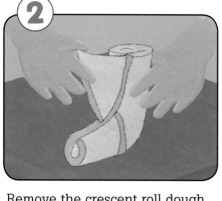

Preheat oven to 375°.

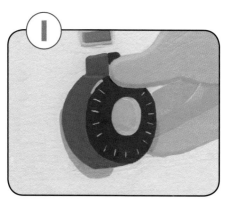

Remove the crescent roll dough from the can. Unroll the dough and separate it into triangles.

Place three pepperoni slices on each triangle.

Sprinkle each triangle with a large pinch of cheese.

HEALTHY CHOICE★ Use sliced mushrooms instead of pepperoni for a vegetarian lunch.

Roll up the triangles and place the rolls, point side down, on a baking sheet.

Ask an adult to bake the rolls for 11 minutes or until golden brown. Remove the rolls from the baking sheet and place them on a serving plate.

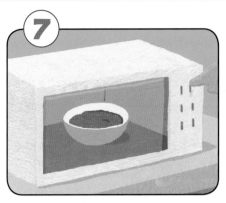

While the rolls are cooling, pour the pizza sauce into a small microwave-safe bowl. Ask an adult to warm the sauce in the microwave for 1 minute.

8 Serve the pizza rolls with warm pizza sauce for dipping.

This Recipe Includes

GRAINS, VEGETABLES, MEAT & BEANS

Tangy Chicken Wraps

INGREDIENTS

1 green bell pepper
Two 6-ounce cans chicken
   breast chunks
1 cup barbecue sauce
4 large flour tortillas
1/4 cup ranch dressing
8 leaves romaine lettuce

TOOLS

Paring knife
Cutting board
Large microwave-safe bowl
Measuring cups
Wooden spoon
Plastic wrap
Measuring spoons

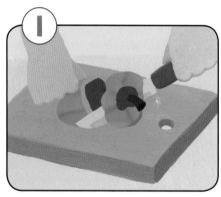

1 Wash the green pepper and have an adult cut off the top. Pull out the seeds and throw them away. Ask an adult to cut the pepper into thin slices.

2 In a large microwave-safe bowl, stir together the chicken, barbecue sauce, and green pepper. Cover the bowl tightly with plastic wrap. Ask an adult to microwave the chicken for 1 1/2 minutes.

3 Wrap the tortillas loosely in plastic wrap. Ask an adult to warm the tortillas in the microwave for 30 seconds.

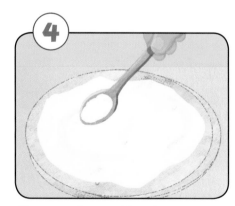

4 Unwrap the tortillas. Layer each tortilla with 1 tablespoon of the ranch dressing, two leaves of lettuce, and one-fourth of the chicken mixture.

5 Tightly roll up each tortilla to make four wraps.

6 Serve.

This Recipe Includes

GRAINS, MILK, MEAT & BEANS

Easy Bean Burritos

INGREDIENTS
8-ounce can refried beans
8 sprigs cilantro
Four 8-inch round flour
   tortillas
1 cup shredded cheddar
   cheese
Sour cream, optional
Salsa, optional

TOOLS
Can opener
Spoon
Small microwave-safe bowl
Plastic wrap
Kitchen shears
Serrated knife
Cutting board
Measuring cups
Measuring spoons

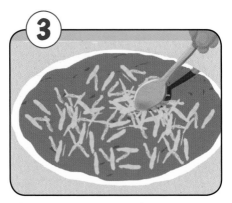

Spoon the beans into a small microwave-safe bowl, and cover with plastic wrap. Ask an adult to heat the beans in the microwave for about 1 minute or until warm.

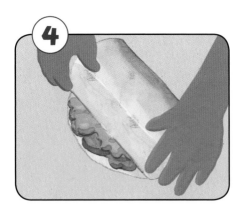

Use the shears to cut the cilantro sprigs into small pieces.

Layer each tortilla with one-fourth of the beans, one-fourth of the cheese, and 1 teaspoon cilantro.

To wrap the burritos, fold one end of the tortilla about 1 inch over the filling. Then fold the left and right sides over the folded end. Finally, fold over the remaining end.

NUTRITION NOTE★ Refried beans are full of protein, which helps build bones, muscles, and skin.

5 Ask an adult to use a serrated knife to slice each burrito in half. Serve with the sour cream and salsa, if desired.

INDEX

ON THE WEB

FactHound offers a safe, fun way to find Web sites related to topics in this book.
All of the sites on FactHound have been researched by our staff.

1. Visit *www.facthound.com*
2. Type in this special code: 1404839992
3. Click on the FETCH IT button.

Your trusty FactHound will fetch the best sites for you!

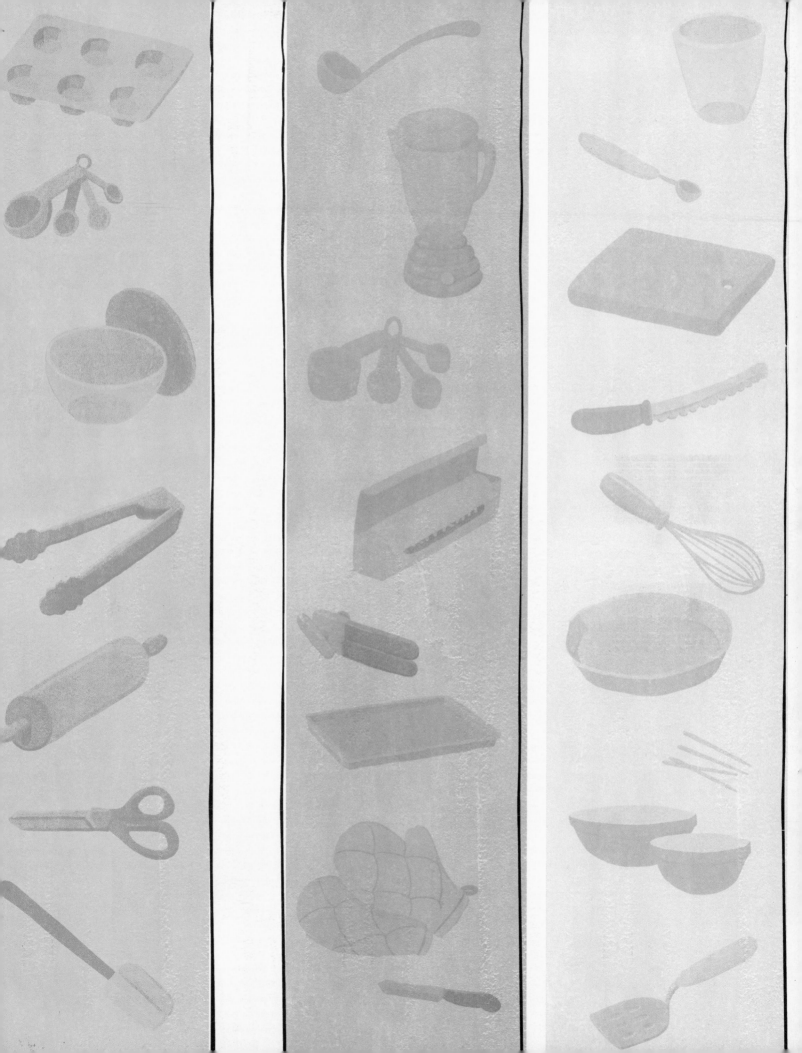

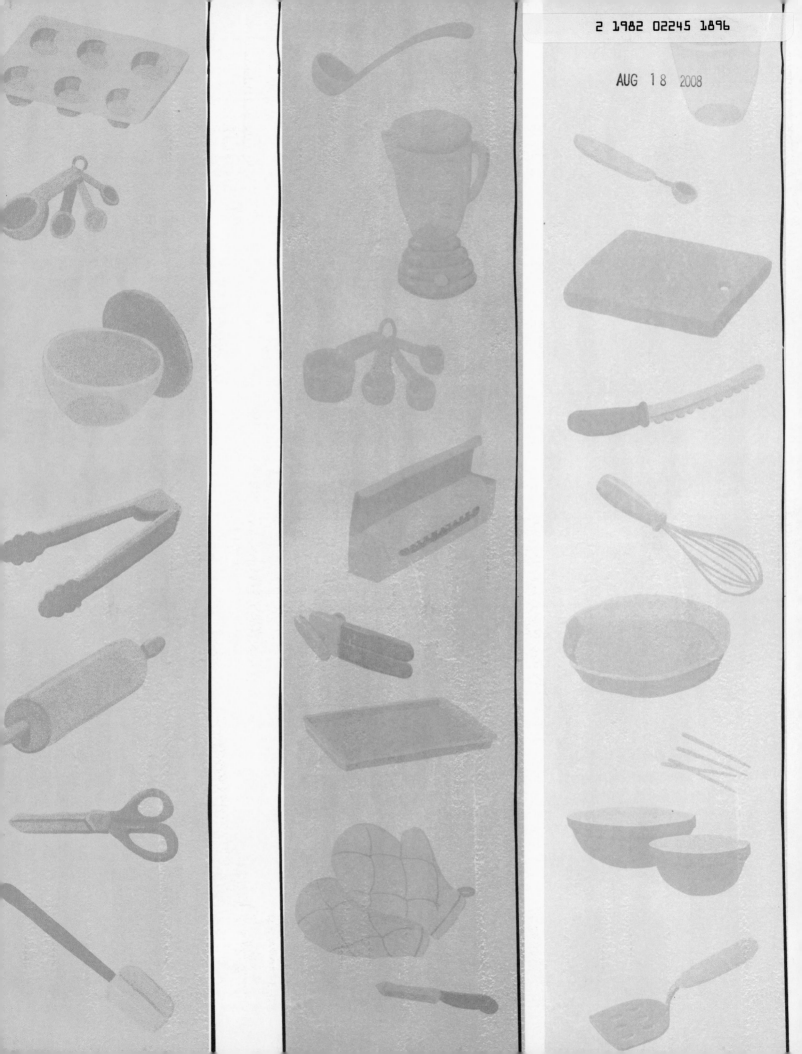